# THE D
# OF TH

## VOL 3: LAND EXPLORATION

### DISCOVERERS

Written and illustrated by
François Place

Translated by Della Denman

MOONLIGHT PUBLISHING

*Something hidden. Go and find it. Go and look
    behind the Ranges —
Something lost behind the Ranges. Lost and
    waiting for you. Go.*

Rudyard Kipling (1865–1936)

# Contents

## EARLY EXPLORERS

**Herodotus** (c.484–425 BC) travelled through the Greek and barbarian world. He left a vivid description of the peoples and places he saw.

**Alexander the Great** (356–323 BC) conquered the Persian Empire which stretched from Greece to India.

**Hsuan-tsang** (600–644) a Chinese Buddhist monk, travelled to India to study and returned home with sacred Buddhist manuscripts.

**Muhammad Al-Idrisi** (1100–1166) was an Arab geographer who travelled through Europe and Asia Minor and made one of the first atlases.

**William of Rubruck** (1220–93), a Flemish missionary, was sent by the French King, Louis IX, to the court of the Grand Khan in Mongolia (1253–5).

**Marco Polo** (1254–1324) was a young Venetian merchant whose book, *The Travels of Marco Polo,* describes his travels along the Silk Road to the court of Genghis Khan.

**Ibn-Battuta** (1304–77) travelled extensively throughout Asia Minor, including Afghanistan, India, the Maldives, Ceylon, Java, Sumatra, China and the Sudan.

## SOUTH AMERICA

■ **Francisco de Orellana** (1511–46) followed Pizarro on an expedition to find cinammon and was the first person to travel down the Amazon (1541).

■ **Vasco Nuñez de Balboa** (1475–1517) was a Spanish conquistador who crossed Panama in 1513 and discovered the 'Great South Sea', the Pacific.

■ **Pedro de Valdivia** (1500–53) took part in the conquest of Peru and then explored and conquered Chile (1540–53).

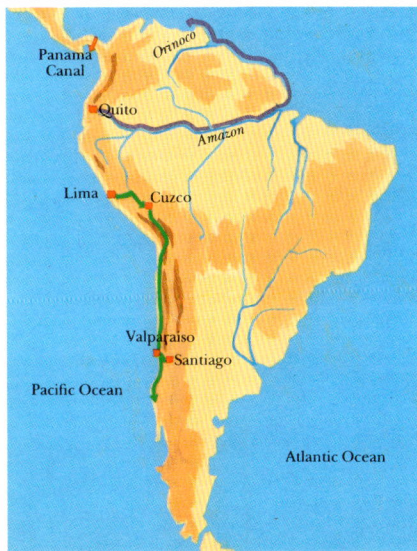

**NORTH AMERICA**
**Hernan Cortes**
(1485–1547)
conquered the Aztec
empire of Mexico
(1519–22).
**Cabeza de Vaca**
(1507–59) survived an
expedition to Florida
and spent eight years
(1528–36) exploring
the southern part of
what is now the
United States.
**Hernando de Soto**
(1500–42) led an
important expedition
from Florida to the
Mississippi (1539–42)
during the course of
which he died.

**Francisco Vasquez de
Coronado** (1510–54)
led reconnaissance
missions in what are
now the states of
Texas, New Mexico
and Arizona.
**Louis Jolliet**
(1645–1700) and
**Jacques Marquette**
(1637–75) explored
the Colbert river (now
the Mississippi).
**Robert Cavelier de
La Salle** (1643–87)
explored Canada and
the Great Lakes Area
(1669–79) and in
1681–2 descended the
Mississippi.

**Alexander
Mackenzie**
(1764–1820) was a
Scotsman who
explored the
Mackenzie river
(1789) and crossed
the Rocky Mountains
reaching the Pacific
Ocean (1792–3).
**Meriwether Lewis**
(1774–1809) and
**William Clark**
(1770–1838) went
from the Mississippi to
the Pacific coast
(1804–6).
**John Charles Fremont**
(1813–90) opened
pioneer routes to
California.

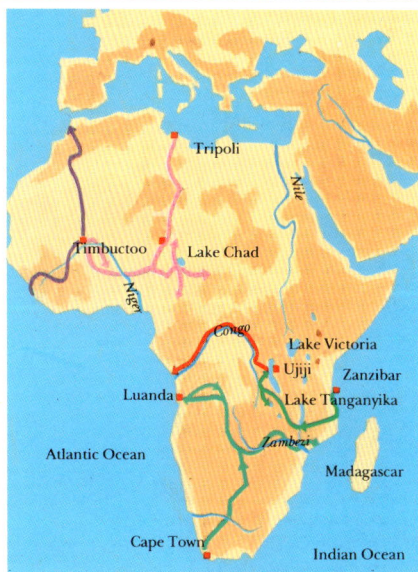

**David Livingstone** (1813–73) travelled throughout the African continent (1840–73). He disappeared in 1866 and was found by Stanley in 1871.

**Henry Morton Stanley** (1841–1904) was a journalist who explored the Great Lakes, the Congo valley, the Ruwenzori and others. He helped found Belgian Congo (Zaïre).

**Pierre Sarvognan de Brazza** (1852–1905) explored Gabon (1876) and Belgian Congo (Zaïre). He helped colonize French Congo (Congo).

## AFRICA
**Leo Africanus** (c.1485–1554) was an Arab geographer and traveller. In 1550 he wrote *A Geographical Description of Africa*.

**Mungo Park** (1771–1806) travelled from Gambia to the Niger River (1795) where he drowned.

**René Caillié** (1799–1838) reached Timbuctoo on 20 April 1828.

**Hugh Clapperton** (1788–1827) explored the Sahara from to Lake Chad (1822–3)

**Heinrich Barth** (1821–65) followed Clapperton's route to Lake Chad and went on to the Niger valley (1850–55).

**Verney Lovett Cameron** (1844–94) went from Zanzibar to the Angolan coast (1873–1875).

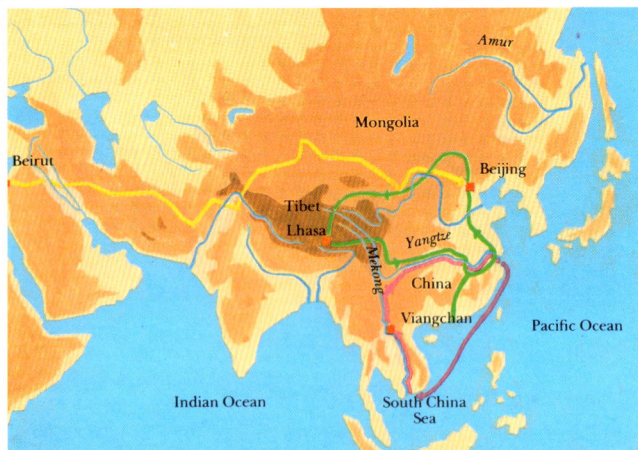

## ASIA

**Semyon Ivanovich Dezhnev** (1605–72) explored Siberia and crossed the Bering Strait (1648).

■ **Evariste-Régis Huc** (1813–60) travelled through Mongolia and Tibet.

**Nicolay Mikhailovich Przhevalsky** (1839–88) explored the Ussuri river (1867–8) and organized four expeditions to central Asia (1870–85).

■ **Francis Garnier** (1839–73) followed the Mekong river and descended the Yangtze (1866–8).

**Sven Hedin** (1865–1952) travelled through Asia and Tibet and made important archaeological finds.

**Charles Haardt** led an automobile ■ caravan across Asia (1931–2).

## SCIENTISTS

**Charles Marie de La Condamine** (1701–74) took part in a scientific expedition to Peru (1735–43) and followed the Amazon to the sea (1743–45).

**Alexander von Humboldt** (1769–1859) explored the tropical areas of America (1799–1804) and later central Asia (1832) with his friend

**Aimé Bonpland** (1773–1858).

**Charles Darwin** (1809–1882) sailed on the *Beagle* (1831–6) collecting scientific data. He stopped in Patagonia, Chile, Peru, the Pacific Islands and Australia. He wrote *On the Origins of the Species* on his return.

## AUSTRALIA

■ **Charles Sturt** (1795–1869) was the first to explore and chart this continent. **Edward Eyre** (1815–1901) ventured into southern Australia (1839–41).

■ **Robert O'Hara Burke** (1820–1861) went from Melbourne to the Gulf of Carpentaria (1860–1). **John Stuart** (1815–66) travelled from south to north various times (1858–62).

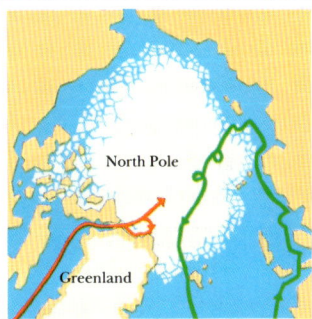

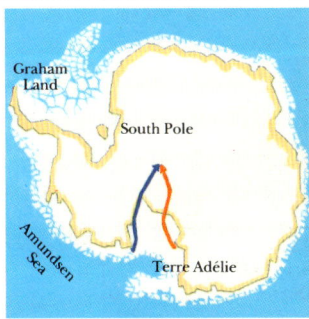

## THE POLES

**Sir John Franklin** (1786–1847) set off on 19 May 1845 to find the north-west passage. He disappeared in July of the same year.

■ **Fridtjof Nansen** (1861–1930) drifted on an ice-floe in his ship *Fram* and then continued by kayak, in an effort to reach the North Pole.
**Adolf Erik Nordenskiöld**

(1832–1901) found the north-east passage in his ship *Vega* (1878–9).
**Sir Ernest Henry Shackleton** (1874–1922) led a party to the South Pole (1907–9) but had to turn back.

■ **Roald Amundsen** (1872–1928) found the north-west passage on his ship *Gjoa* (1903–6). He was the first explorer to reach the South Pole (14 December 1911).

■ **Robert Edwin Peary** (1856–1920) proved that Greenland is an island (1900). His daughter was born on the expedition. He reached the North Pole on 7 April 1909

■ **Robert Falcon Scott** (1868–1912) led numerous expeditions to Antarctica. He reached the South Pole on 16 January 1912 and died on the return journey.

# Herodotus

## A Greek traveller, 3RD century BC

An Egyptian scribe with papyrus. He is drawn in profile in the typical Egyptian manner.

The pyramids of Giza were already over a thousand years old when Herodotus was alive.

*I shall spend longer on Egypt as it holds more wonders than any other land and contains so much to admire that it defies description.*
Herodotus

Food to sustain the dead in their afterlife was often pictured on the walls of tombs.

## Ancient Egypt observed

Herodotus was one of the greatest travellers of all time. Born in Asia Minor about 480 BC, he spent most of his life exploring the lands around the Mediterranean, which to the Greeks of the time made up the known world. He described them in his nine-volume journal.

Herodotus can be considered the world's first historian. His books analyse the historical links between the peoples of the Mediterranean and describe the wars between the Greeks and the Persians, the first recorded confrontation between West and East.

He tells us in detail about the marvels of ancient Egyptian civilisation. He describes their religion, laws, customs and architecture.

Trawling for fish on the Nile, Egypt's famous life-giving river

Irrigation methods used by farmers along the banks of the Nile have developed little since the time of Herodotus.

The Scythians hunting on horseback on the plains of the Ukraine. Herodotus says: *They are excellent archers, even on horseback, and their homes are their chariots.*

### Scythians

The writings of Herodotus were for centuries the only source of information on the Scythians, nomadic horsemen who lived on the steppes of what is now the Ukraine. His descriptions of their funerary rites tally exactly with archaeological excavations carried out more than 2,000 years later.

His accounts of lands on the borders and beyond the known world were less precise. Often cut off by

Detail of a Scythian necklace. The horse and rider are the favourite motifs of Scythian jewellers

The royal sceptre of a Persian dynasty

The walls of Babylon

deserts, swamps and mountains the peoples who lived there became the stuff of myth and legend.

An excellent storyteller, Herodotus kept his readers' interest awake with amusing stories, dialogues and even speeches by the leading historical figures. He was a great traveller with an eye for detail and a real interest in the customs of the places he visited. Of Babylon, Herodotus commented: 'It is so magnificent that no other town can be compared with it.'

Of Libya, he said: 'Beyond the maritime coast and the countries which border it is a land of wild beasts. And beyond this land is just sand, prodigiously arid and absolutely deserted.'

People of the marshes of the river Euphrates

A Nubian. Nubia stretches south, beyond the first cataract of the Nile.

The Libyan desert

# Voyage to India

## Hsuan-tsang, AD 629–645

The routes to the West are dangerous, said Hsuan-tsang: 'Sometimes you are stopped by searing winds, quicksands, or demons. When you come across them you cannot escape.'

A Chinese pilgrim monk with his *kakkhara* (stick) and *sutra* (manuscripts).

Buddhism developed in India and was slowly spread to China by the merchants and missionaries who travelled the Silk Road. The golden age of this religion in China lasted from the 6th to the 8th century. Many monks made the long pilgrimage from China to India. The best known was Hsuantsang who set off in 629 at the age of 26. He returned 17 years later having covered nearly 30,000 kms. Among the great dangers he overcame was the terrible Gobi desert where he nearly died of thirst.

### The Silk Road

Hsuan-tsang followed the caravan route to Samarkand. He then crossed Afghanistan, spent some time in Kashmir and finally reached India.

Nearly everywhere he went he was warmly welcomed by the local rulers. They were so impressed with his wisdom they showered him with gifts and presented him with escorts.

Huan-tsang studied under the best teachers at Nalanda, the cultural centre of the Buddhist world. Then he returned triumphantly to China where he spent the rest of his life poring over precious sacred texts which he translated into Chinese. His memoirs recount his marvellous journeys.

Chortens: travellers had to pass to the left of these sacred monuments.

A giant statue of Buddha hewn from the rock

# Among the Mongols

## William of Rubruck, 1253–1255

William of Rubruck was one of the first Europeans to cross the vast uncharted lands of central Asia. In his lively account of the two-year journey, he described the geography of the steppes and the customs of the nomadic Mongol tribes who lived there.

William, a Franciscan friar, left the Holy Land in 1253 as an emissary of the French king, St Louis. France was fighting in the Holy Land in the last of the crusades against the Muslims. St Louis was seeking allies and hoped that the Mongols might be favourable to the Christian cause.

The mission failed but William

The king of France, Louis IX, was made a saint after his death for his involvement in the Crusades.

returned home with much valuable information on the lifestyles of the people of central Asia about whom little was known.

On his way to the court of the Grand Khan or chief of the Mongols, William crossed the immense steppes to the north of the Black Sea. When he arrived everything astounded him. 'While I was among them I seemed to be in another world', he commented.

He was particularly impressed with Chinese ideograms and was the first to write about them: 'The Chinese write with a brush which resembles a painter's brush. Each of the characters they paint denotes a whole world.'

*The cold is such that it cracks rocks and even trees.*

A Mongol encampment

Chinese ideograms

# Marco Polo

## The discovery of China, 1271–1295

Venetian trading vessels

Travellers believed the deserts were inhabited by evil and monstrous spirits.

Marco Polo was only 17 years old when in 1271 he began his long journey to the end of the world. He went with his father and his uncle, both merchants from Venice, who had seen the court of the grand Khan on a previous visit to Cathay (China).

Fifty years earlier the Mongol tribes had laid waste the vast plains of central Asia, sweeping aside secular kingdoms and weakening Islamic power. Now, however, the traditional commercial routes such as the Silk Road were in use again.

### On the Silk Road

The three travellers followed the caravan routes which crossed the Karman desert, the Badakshan mountains, the high passes of Kashmir, the Gobi desert, and the steppes of Mongolia. They finally reached Cambaluc, the capital of the great Mongol ruler, Kublai Khan.

*You have to travel a good forty days between Greece and the Levant, over mountains, along coasts, through valleys, past waterfalls, and across deserts. In all these forty days you will not see a single dwelling or inn so travellers have to take everything they need with them.*
Marco Polo

Huge shaggy cattle were a common sight on Marco Polo's route: they were yaks.

*The city has twelve gates and over each gate there is a great and handsome palace. The streets are so straight and wide that you can see right along them from end to end and from one gate to another.*
Marco Polo

## The stay in China

The three Venetians were received by Kublai Khan who was immediately impressed with Marco Polo's vitality and sense of purpose. He entrusted the young man with assignments throughout his empire.

Marco Polo, like all Venetians, was primarily a merchant and was fascinated by the prosperity of Chinese towns and the far-reaching, highly developed trading system.

Other aspects of Chinese life he admired were the use of paper money and coal, the postal system with its 300,000 horses, and the huge rivers teeming with boats and crossed by wondrous bridges.

At Kublai Khan's court the young traveller took part in sumptuous celebrations, in hunts with armies of beaters, and in banquets attended by thousands of guests.

The Khan's postal system used relays of horses and covered enormous distances.

## The return home

The three Venetians amassed a fortune thanks to the patronage of the Khan. But when he died they became concerned about their future and decided to leave China.

At the first chance they converted their riches into precious stones and offered to escort a Mongol princess to her wedding in Persia. The journey on to Venice was long and difficult. Only by disguising themselves as beggars were they able to cross the war-torn Middle East.

In Venice Marco Polo became involved in the conflict between Venice and Genoa. He was taken prisoner. Behind bars he dictated to his cell-

A wine fountain
in the court of
the Khan

Chinese junks

mate the story of his travels which we can now read as *The Travels of Marco Polo*.

In his book, Marco Polo described Levant on the high seas 1,500 miles from land'. The inhabitants, he said, had so much gold they did not know what to do with it.

The book was an immediate success. So informative a guide was it that Christopher Columbus took a carefully annotated copy on his first journey to America. He thought it might help in his search for a new maritime route to the Indies.

Harvesting pepper
*In these islands there grows both white and black pepper in great abundance.*
Marco Polo

The collecting of pearls and precious stones for the Grand Khan, the wealthiest man on earth, according to Marco Polo.

# Travels through Islam

## Ibn-Battuta, 1325–1354

Arab dhow

A typical Arab
fortified town

Ibn Battuta, a Moroccan, was an indefatigable traveller of the Islamic world. In over thirty years of incessant journeying he covered 100,000 kms from the Red Sea to Zanzibar, from Persia to the Indies, from China to Sumatra, from Spain to the heart of the Sahara.

He explored more territory than Marco Polo and his accurate yet colourful accounts give a vivid picture of the cultural and commercial links between Arabia, the African coast, and the Far East.

Like most educated Arabs of his time Ibn Battuta undertook the pilgrimage to Mecca at the age of 20.

He was 50 before he returned to his native town, Tangiers.

Ibn Battuta's adventures are as exciting as the stories recounted in *The Thousand and One Nights*.

At one stage he was a pilgrim in Arabia, at another an ambassador and a counsellor to the fearful Sultan of Delhi. He was shipwrecked, he was made a chieftain in the Maldive Islands, he was jailed, he was married and divorced several times.

He experienced honour and disgrace, wealth and extreme poverty. And his knowledge and skill as a raconteur earnt him friends everywhere.

Arab hospitality

The coconut is a rich source of nutrition in the tropics.

Arab pilgrims

# Discovering the Pacific

## Vasco Nuñez de Balboa, 1513

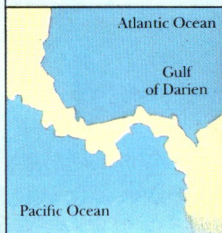

Atlantic Ocean

Gulf
of Darien

Pacific Ocean

A line of Spanish
soldier-explorers
(*conquistadores*)
in the dense jungle

Vasco Nuñez de Balboa was the first European explorer to see the Pacific Ocean. He sailed for the American continent in 1501 and became governor of a small Spanish colony on the Darien Gulf.

He was a ruthless and avaricious leader who bullied the local Indians and extorted their gold.

Finally, to satisfy his greed, the Indians told him of 'an immense sea to the south'. He set off in 1513 with an expedition of 186 men. Cutting their way through the virgin forest, killing and looting as they went, they marched for 27 days until they saw the limitless horizon of the Pacific.

His triumph was short-lived. Complaints about him had reached the Spanish king and in 1519 he was executed.

*Indians being eaten alive by the dogs of the* conquistadores

*Balboa and his men claiming possession of the Pacific Ocean in the name of the present and future kings of Spain*

# The Amazon

Journeys into the interior, 1539–1542

A gold figurine from Columbia

The myth of Eldorado (the word comes from *hombre dorado* meaning golden man) derived from a Colombian rite during which a man covered himself in gold dust and plunged into the lake. The *conquistadores* came to believe that Eldorado was a country of fabulous wealth where everything was made of gold.

In 1539 a *conquistador* expedition set out from Quito in search of cinnamon and the legendary Eldorado. It was headed by Gonzalo Pizarro, whose brother Francisco had conquered the Incas.

**In search of Eldorado**

After a year of preparations the expedition set off eastward. The small team of Spaniards was followed by thousands of porters, mules and llamas, while heavily laden carts carried provisions.

The party wound its way down the Andean foothills and entered the vast forest just as the rainy season was starting. Before long disease and the terrible conditions they encountered had taken a heavy toll and Pizarro ordered his second-in-command, a half-blind officer called Francisco de Orellana, to carry on with a reduced force.

In a vain attempt to find the secret of Eldorado the *conquistadores* tortured the natives. They were directed further and further into the jungle until they emerged from the undergrowth at the mouth of a huge river. It was the Amazon.

The arrival, in 1542, of the Spanish *conquistadores* at the mouth of the vast river which they named the Amazon, after the warrior-women they had come across in the forest.

The *conquistadores* identified the women warriors with the Amazons of Greek mythology.

*These women are very white, very tall, strong and almost completely naked. Armed with a bow and arrows some of them fight as well as ten Indians.*
From an account of the expedition

# The conquest of Chile

## 1540–1553

A figurine in baked clay

In 1540 an immense expedition led by Pedro de Valdivia set off from Peru across the Andes mountains towards what is now Chile. It consisted of 150 Spaniards, over 1,000 Indian porters, craftsmen, hundreds of llamas, horses and mules, and all kinds of livestock from cattle to chickens. This expedition was not only a voyage of discovery but a colonising force.

A preliminary expedition led by Diego de Almagro had left in the same direction five years earlier. It had come to grief among the frozen passes of the Andes and the arid stretches of the Atacama desert. The route taken by Valdivia's men was lined with the bleached skeletons of Almagro's soldiers.

Valdivia's better-equipped expedition survived the hardships of the journey and reached the Pacific Ocean. He founded the city of Valparaiso (Paradise Valley) in a verdant valley dotted with almond trees, and then, further inland, Santiago, giving the Spanish crown a huge new territory: Chile.

In 1547 Valdivia returned to Peru and was appointed governor of Chile. He organized a further expedition in 1550, with the aim of penetrating the South. The local Arucanian indians bitterly resented this invading force and attacked his army repeatedly. Finally in 1553 they succeeded in killing Valdivia.

The condor, sacred bird of the Incas, gliding over the Andes

Valdivia's huge expedition wending its way across the Andes

# The Mississippi

Hernando de Soto, 1539–1542

In the swamps of Florida, de Soto's men were often attacked by Seminol Indians, masters of the art of ambush.

Peru and Mexico had already been claimed for the Spanish crown when Hernando de Soto set out on a voyage of discovery to the north. He hoped to find gold and fabulous treasures in these uncharted territories but he was to be bitterly disappointed.

In 1539, de Soto landed in Florida at the head of a well-armed force.

While the Indians carried only bows and arrow and clubs, the Spanish soldiers were equipped with protective helmets and breastplates and carried swords and muskets.

The Spaniards had to contend with alligators and poisonous snakes in the swamplands, and the fierce Seminol and Comanche Red Indian tribes before reaching the Appalachians.

In 1542 they finally arrived at 'the father of rivers', the Mississippi. There was no gold or treasure but the demoralised forces were able to establish a settlement.

On 21 May, however, de Soto was struck down by fever. In order to prevent his body being mauled by Indians it was placed in a hollow tree trunk and floated downstream.

The Indian pueblos or fortified villages gave the impression of great hidden wealth.

Forerunners of the horse had existed and died out in the Americas. It was the *conquistadores* who introduced the modern horse there.

# Canada to Louisiana

Cavelier de la Salle, 1681–1682

A small trading post used by fur traders in the Canadian forest

A pink flamingo from the delta of the Mississippi

After the founding of Quebec in 1608 many French people went to Nouvelle France (Canada) to seek their fortunes. Robert Cavelier de la Salle arrived in 1666 from Normandy. He learned several Indian languages and travelled huge distances by canoe or on foot seeking new routes for the fur trade.

An Indian smoking a peace pipe

A swift and silent Indian canoe

His explorations took him to the Great Lakes, which he sailed in his ship *Le griffon*, and to Illinois, the homeland of the fierce Iroquois Indians.

## Descending the Mississippi

At the beginning of 1682 the intrepid Frenchman took twenty of his companions and a group of loyal Mohican Indians and travelled the length of the Mississippi. Arriving at the delta on April 6, they formally took possession of the whole area, calling it Louisiana in honour of the king of France.

A European fort in North America

On the banks of the Mississippi

# The far North

Alexander Mackenzie, 1789–1793

A trapper

In North America when exploration and commerce were inseparable, Alexander Mackenzie, a young Canadian of Scots origin, worked for the North West Company, the main fur traders. In 1789 he was the commander of a fort on Lake Athabasca on the edge of uncharted territory; his ambition was to discover a navigable route for the fur trade west to Asia.

## River of Disappointment

On 3 June Mackenzie left his fort by canoe with a handful of men, hoping to reach the west coast of Alaska. He travelled from river to lake, and lake to river, but to his bitter disappointment found that the river flowed north to the Arctic ocean. When he arrived at its mouth he christened it River of Disappointment. It now bears his name.

Four years later Mackenzie was still determined to attain his goal and mounted a second expedition. He finally reached the Pacific Ocean on 22 July 1793. This made him the first European to cross the North American land mass.

The Canadian North was a huge game reserve for trappers.

Crossing the Rocky Mountains Mackenzie and his team had to negotiate surging rapids.

# The route to the West

## Lewis and Clark, 1804–1806

Canoeing through canyons

At the beginning of the 19th century a large part of North America was still unknown: *terra incognita*. Only the trappers had ventured east of the Missouri. Thomas Jefferson, the third president of the United States, decided to organise an expedition from the Mississippi to the Pacific to assess natural resources and to draw up a precise topographical survey, a record of the natural land features. He also wanted to know if the local Indian tribes were friendly.

Unlike the Black Foot the Mandan Indians were friendly towards white men.

A Missouri tribal village under snow

Captains Meriwether Lewis and William Clark were selected for the mission. Their indispensable guides were a Shoshoni woman called Sacajawea and her husband, the French trader Toussaint Charbonneau.

The expedition covered 6,600 kms in two years. It crossed the Rockies, followed the Snake and Columbia rivers, and finally reached the Pacific.

The route to the West was finally open to pioneers.

Thanks to Sacajawea the expedition bought ponies from the Shoshoni tribe in order to cross the Rockies.

# Scientific exploration

## Charles de la Condamine, 1735–1742

Passing through a Peruvian village

La Condamine published a treatise on rubber in 1751.

In the 18th century it was scientific curiosity rather than commercial gain that spurred on men of learning to the ends of the earth.

The French Academy of Science decided to send missions to Lapland and the equator to measure the earth's meridian (half of its circumference, passing through the poles) and to establish the exact shape of the planet.

In 1735 a scientific expedition set sail for Peru. On board were three members of the Academy and Charles Marie de la Condamine, a distinguished young scholar of mathematics, physics, and medicine.

It took nearly seven years to complete their assignments and reports.

**The Amazon: a perilous green jungle**

In 1743 the members of the expedition took separate routes home.

La Condamine had already climbed several volcanoes in the Andes. Now he decided to go down the Amazon and chart its course. During this perilous venture he discovered that the two great basins of the Amazon and the Orinoco were connected by a complex network of tributaries.

On 27 September after two months in this so-called 'green nightmare', he arrived in Cayenne on the Atlantic coast with enough information to write a detailed report which greatly increased European knowledge of South America.

An indian with a blowpipe in the Amazon jungle. La Condamine studied the vegetable poisons, such as curare, which the tribesmen used on the tips of their arrows.

A religious settlement beside the Amazon. Many priests travelled to the new world to convert the Indians to the Catholic faith.

# The Orinoco

Humboldt and Bonpland, 1799–1804

Volcanoes of mud

In 1799 the German scientist Alexander von Humboldt and his French friend, Aimé Bonpland, left for Cumana in Venezuela. For these two highly knowledgeable young scholars it was the beginning of a great adventure which took them from the Amazonian forest to Cuba, from the volcanoes of Peru to the Aztec ruins in Mexico.

**Intrepid explorers**

They wended their way down the Orinoco to its source in a dug-out canoe, braving the mosquitoes and the terrible humidity of the tropical forests. They came across many dangerous animals including jaguars.

Despite these difficulties they succeeded in recording 12,000 plant specimens and were the first naturalists to explore this river basin.

A heavily loaded dug-out canoe

In Peru they crossed dizzying heights on makeshift bridges, negotiated narrow gorges, and suffered extremes of temperatures. Thanks to Humboldt's mountaineering skills they were able to climb 5,791 metres up Chimborazo in Ecuador, a height never reached before.

Humboldt's findings gained him recognition from scientists throughout Europe and after his return home in 1804, he published several works. All in all the expedition had collected 60,000 plant specimens, about 6,000 of which were unknown to science. It took Humboldt 25 years to produce the thirty-four volumes which charted his findings.

A cacajao monkey

Humboldt and Bonpland collecting plants in Mexico

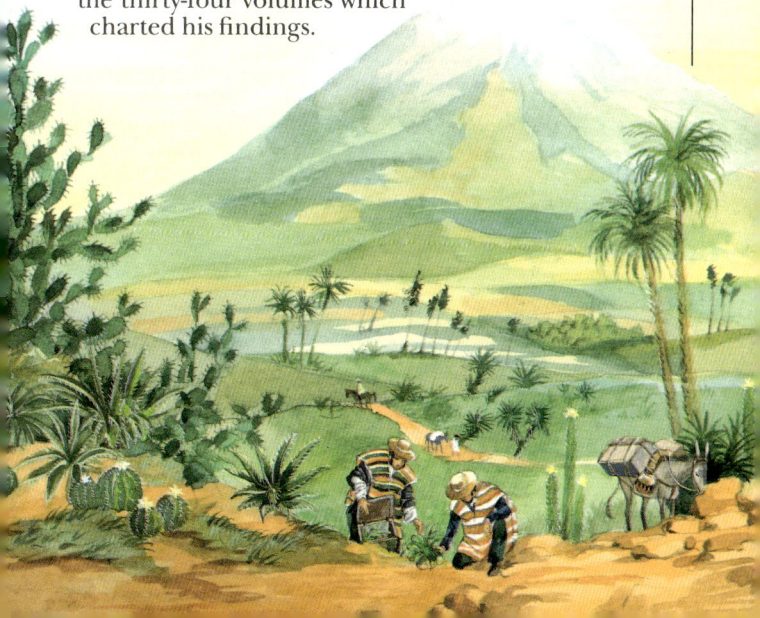

# Charles Darwin

## 1831–1836

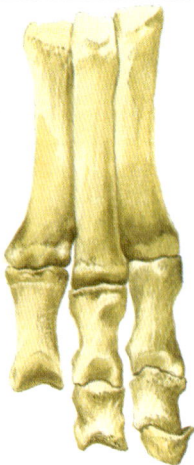

Bones discovered at Punta Alta on the coast of Argentina

In 1831 a British vessel, the *Beagle*, started out on a voyage of exploration around the world. On board was a keen 22-year old naturalist, Charles Darwin. From the beginning it was clear he had brilliant gifts of observation.

On the American continent his curiosity took him far into the interior, into equatorial forest, and into Argentinian pampas lands where he lived with the gauchos, the part-Indian horseman and herdsmen.

The fossils he discovered in Patagonia encouraged him to study the geographical history of the Earth.

In the Andes the petrified forests and the layers of prehistoric shells at an altitude of 4,000 metres suggested vast movements in the earth's crust, in the past.

In the Galapagos islands Darwin had noted that certain animal species evolved in different ways on each island. This was the inspiration for his revolutionary work *On the Origin of the Species by Means of Natural Selection*, published in 1859.

It gave an alternative to the biblical version of the history of the Earth and the creation of man.

Chasing rheas, the ostriches of S. America, in the Argentine pampas

A sea lizard or iguana of the Galapagos islands. The differences between sea and land lizards illustrated how members of the same species adapted to different conditions.

The *Beagle* moored while Darwin collected specimens on shore

# The myth of Timbuctoo

## René Caillié, 1826–1828

The baobab tree has been described as the 'upside-down' tree.

Timbuctoo, the mysterious capital of a former wealthy African kingdom, was a Muslim sanctuary banned to Europeans at the beginning of the 19th century. One Englishman, Gordon Laing, who had reached the forbidden city in 1826 was brutally murdered.

René Caillié had dreamt of travelling since his orphaned childhood in France and was determined to visit Timbuctoo. He embarked on his mission in Senegal where he learnt the Arab language and familiarised himself with Muslim customs.

In 1827, disguised as an Arab, he joined a caravan which was heading towards the Niger. He was robbed, manhandled, weakened by scurvy,

Arab bandits attacking a north African village in order to enforce tribute from it.

The banks of the Niger

and reduced to begging, but finally reached his goal in 1828.

What he found was 'nothing but a mass of ill-looking houses built of earth.' Timbuctoo had been stripped of its splendour. Penniless and exhausted, Caillié joined a return caravan. On reaching Paris he was awarded the Gold Medal by the French Geographical Society for his exploits. He wrote a riveting and detailed account of his travels but was hailed as a fraud by the British and died unknown.

The towns of the Niger were adapted to the climate and built of dry earth.

A Fulani from Fouta Djallon

# The Sahara

## Heinrich Barth, 1850–1855

In the Sahara Barth found rock paintings which showed that the desert was once fertile

In 1850 a small caravan left Tripoli in Libya to explore the desert lands of the Sahara and the Sudan. Heinrich Barth, a knowledgeable young German scientist, spoke Arabic and was acquainted with Islamic traditions, essential skills in a land foreign to Christians.

He was regarded as a gentleman of learning by princes who had grown rich through slave-trading, a practice that he was against. But he was grateful for their friendship and protection. They saved his life many times.

High winds in the Sahara, the Arabs' 'inland sea'

The expedition travelled through areas devastated by war and pillaging. Barth visited Agadez (now central Niger), Lake Chad, and Timbuctoo where he stayed for about nine months.

He travelled a total distance of 16,000 kms, usually without any European companions and with little cash. His diary of the journey is a mine of vital information on areas previously almost unknown.

A village chief bargaining with Moorish slave traders.

An audience with the Sultan of Bornu who was protected by an army of horsemen.

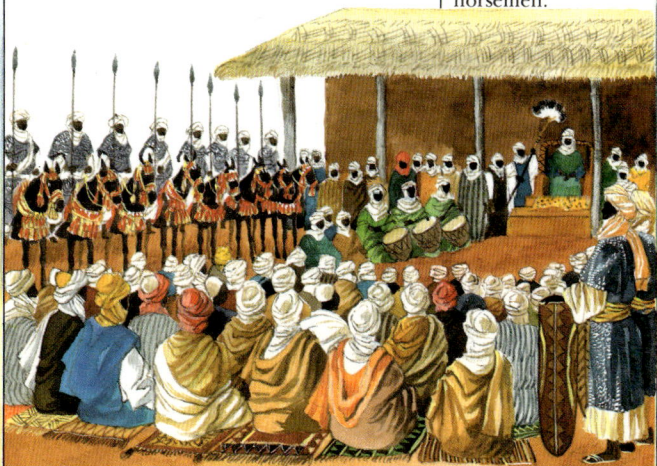

# David Livingstone

In the heart of Africa, 1840–1873

The African interior was still a blank on world maps when David Livingstone, a Scottish medical missionary, first set foot on the continent in 1841, in Cape Town.

His aims were to fight the Arab slave trade and to open up Africa to Christian missionaries, and he devoted the rest of his life to its exploration.

By 1842 he had gone further into the Kalahari desert than any other white man and was proving to be an explorer of exceptional stamina and endurance.

Victoria Falls

In 1856 he was the first European to see the Victoria falls.

The fame Livingstone won from early trips enabled him to mount further expeditions in the hope of finding the source of the Nile. He discovered Lake Nyasa and Lake Tanganyika, and made a stand against slave trafficking.

Livingstone's historic meeting with Henry Stanley took place on 10 November 1871. The explorer had contracted a fever and in Europe was feared dead. Stanley, an American reporter, found him at Ujiji on Lake Tanganyika. Livingstone died two years later.

Livingstone was fascinated by African wildlife like gnu.

'Dr Livingstone, I presume?'
'Yes,' he replied.
'Thank God I have found you.'

Dugs-outs on a lake. Beware of the hippos!

# Henry Morton Stanley

## A reporter turns explorer, 1870–1877

Stanley travelled in style and controlled his army of porters and native guides with a military discipline. He also learnt how to market himself, quoting his sponsors and suppliers in his reports.

When Stanley began his search for Livingstone he already had a sound reputation as a globe-trotting journalist for the *New York Herald Tribune*. He was in Madrid covering the Spanish Civil War when in 1869 the paper sent him to search for the missing Livingstone. As soon as Stanley arrived on the black continent he discovered his vocation as an explorer.

Having found Livingstone, the keen reporter obtained his newspaper's approval to continue his exploration of equatorial Africa.

### Perilous descent

He planned to cross equatorial Africa, from Zanzibar to the mouth of the Congo on the Atlantic coast. Travelling downstream, mainly by dug-out canoe, Stanley and his men braved rapids, storms and attacks from cannibal tribes. After 1,700 kms they finally reached the ocean in 1877.

Collapsible steel boat

# Mongolia and Tibet

Huc and Gabet, 1844–1846

Huc and Gabet were two French monks who had been instructed by their father superior to establish a mission in central Asia. 'You must travel from tent to tent, from people to people,' he had said, 'until Providence shows you the place where you must stop.'

The two men crossed the steppes of Mongolia. They dressed in native clothes and slept in tents or in the open air alongside nomadic tribes. Sometimes people asked them to read horoscopes which they believed would help them find stray or stolen animals!

In 1845 the monks joined the imposing caravan of the Tibetan embassy

Caravans were sometimes attacked by Tibetan bandits. 'They were armed with huge swords which hung from either side of their belts and had a rifle slung across their back. They had black shoulder-length hair, wolf-skin bonnets, and wild eyes.'

The Tibetan embassy's long caravan crossing a snowy pass

returning home from Peking to Lhasa. The route was long and arduous, through snow-covered passes and across glaciers. Gabet had to be strapped to his camel to prevent him falling off with exhaustion.

The following year they arrived in Lhasa. Few foreigners had been to this isolated and exotic city before. They were warmly welcomed by the Tibetans but the Chinese official was hostile to them and had them expulsed after a brief stay.

Lhasa is dominated by the Potala, the palace of the Dalai Lama.

The Buddhist monks blow radungs or giant trumpets.

# The conquest of Siberia

In the 16th century the Russians were curious to explore the vast territory extending east of the Ural mountains.

In 1581 Maxime Stroganov, the head of a wealthy dynasty of merchants, and Yermak, the famous chief of a band of Cossacks, crossed the Urals and overcame the Tartars, the people of Eastern Asia. They thus opened up a way into Siberia.

Over the following years the Cossacks, who came from southern Russia between the Black and the Caspian seas, continued to be the driving force behind the conquest of the east. In 1648 they advanced to the Pacific and reached the Bering Strait, seventy years before its official discovery.

The seemingly endless forests of

Iakoute      Tchouktche      Kamtchadales

the taiga of Siberia provided rich pickings for gold diggers and fur traders. The trappers hunted bears and wolves, foxes and sables, otters and stoats. In the Arctic waters the Cossacks hunted walrus for its valuable ivory tusks.

The conquest of Siberia was completed with the construction of the Trans-Siberian railway in the 19th century. It then became possible to travel by rail all the way from China to Russia.

A detachment of Cossacks emerging from the Siberian forest

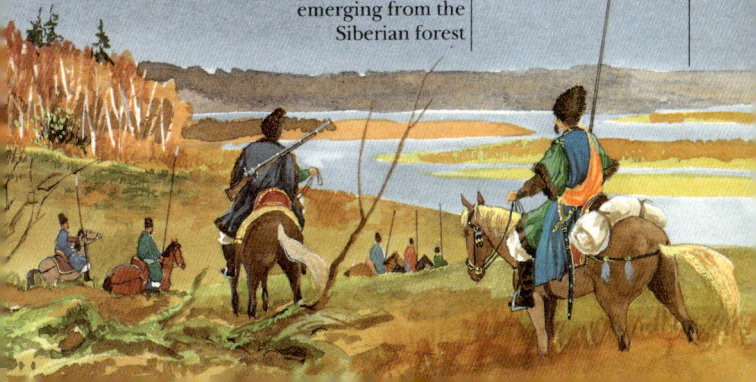

The people of Siberia were skilled hunters.

*They wear costly furs, such as ermine, squirrel and black fox. Being excellent hunters they have outstanding selections of pelts.*

Marco Polo

# The Mekong river

## 1866–1868

A Mandarin,
an important
official in
China and
Indo-China

A flooded road in Laos

The Mekong is the longest river in Indochina. Its source is in Tibet but it runs through part of China, Laos, and Cambodia and ends in a delta in the south of Vietnam

In 1866 a French expedition set out to chart the course of the Mekong and explore the possibility of opening a commercial route between China and France's colony, Vietnam.

The expedition was under the leadership of Doudart de Lagrée, with

Francis Garnier as second in command. Garnier was allowed to leave the main party and undertake some explorations of his own.

Alone and on foot he travelled the 1,600 kms to Angkor Vat, a magnificent complex of temples of the ancient Khmer civilization, where he made important archaeological finds.

Rejoining the expedition he found Lagrée dying and, taking over command, brought the journey to a successful end following the Yangtze to Shanghai. They were the first Europeans, since Marco Polo, to chart the course of the Yangtze river so far from the sea.

Fighting against the rapids

Passing through a village in Laos

# The Haardt expedition

1931

With the development of cars, drivers became fascinated by the idea of exploring the old caravan routes. The ancient and impracticable Silk Road was seen as one such challenge.

In 1931 a group of Frenchmen, led by Charles Haardt and Victor Point, decided to drive the thousands of miles between Beirut and Beijing. Two teams were formed, to start from opposite ends of the proposed route and meet half way. They travelled in caterpillar lorries designed to cope with all terrains.

Only one contingent made it to Kashgar, in central Asia, for the meeting. Nonetheless the perseverance of the teams has gone down in the annals of motoring history.

In the deserts of central Asia

From the Lebanon to Afghanistan the teams were warmly welcomed by the local people.

The courageous drivers had to cross fragile bridges over gorges and contend with roads carried away by rains or blocked by snow. The China group braved the sandstorms and the fearsome warlords of the Gobi desert.

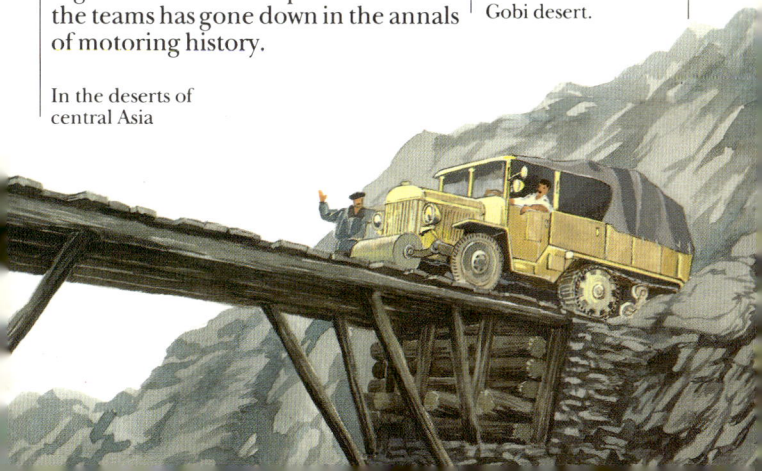

# Crossing Australia

## 1860–1871

The first British settlers arrived at Port Jackson on the south-east coast of Australia in 1788. Only part of the Australian coast had been charted by Captain Cook and a small area of rich pasture-land along the coast was known to Europeans.

The heart of the continent, a semi-desert, seemed impenetrable. Rivers simply disappeared into the desert sands.

In 1860 an expedition led by Robert Burke left Melbourne with the aim of crossing the continent from south to north. It was the first time that dromedaries, the 'ships of the desert', had been used in Australia. Burke and two of his party reached what appeared to be an estuary but were halted by dense mangrove swamps. They had made the vital link between south and north

An Aborigine. It is said that the Aborigines have lived in Australia for 40,000 years.

and arrived at the mouth of the Flinders river on the Gulf of Carpenteria.

The return journey was tragic. The heat of the desert, thirst and hunger killed all but one of the expedition. He was saved by Aborigines.

In 1860 a second attempt was made, led by John Stuart. The expedition travelled from Adelaide to Arnhern Land and back, but the exhausted and blinded Stuart had to be carried home by colleagues.

In 1871 a telegraph link was established between Adelaide on the south coast and Darwin on the north coast. This in turn was connected by an underwater cable to Indonesia.

Fast-moving kangaroos provided an unusual prey for the English settlers.

Imagine the surprise of the settlers to see this strange bounding animal carrying its young in its pouch.

# The North Pole
## 1909

A ship trapped in the ice-floe

Essentials for a polar expedition were sledges and dogs.

Since the 16th century navigators had been intent on finding two new routes to the North Pole – the Northwest passage following the coast of Canada and Alaska, and the Northeast passage north of the Siberian coast.

Polar exploration only became possible in the 19th century. And what drew attention to this immense icy wasteland was the loss of and the long and fruitless search for the Franklin expedition and its two ships, which disappeared between 1845 and 1848.

At first it was unclear whether

the wasteland was a continent or merely frozen ice. But the drifting of an American vessel, the *Jeannette*, trapped in an ice-floe from 1881 to 1884 left no doubt that it was an ocean.

During the 1890s explorers and adventurers initiated a new sport, approaching the North Pole on skis. A young Norwegian, Fridtjof Nansen, made the first attempt in 1895. He had already deliberately let his ship drift on an ice-floe near Greenland and skied there. His attempt at the North Pole was a challenge to others.

The official discoverer of the North Pole was Robert Edwin Peary, an American naval officer. He surveyed the Arctic peninsula and made three attempts to reach the Pole, succeeding in 1909. He moored his ship, the *Roosevelt*, off Ellesmere Island (north of Greenland) and travelled by sledge and on foot. He reached the Pole on 6 April and made a sounding through the ice but found no bottom.

The polar bear, an excellent swimmer with a powerful swipe, was dreaded by polar explorers.

An explorer wearing a fur costume adapted to arctic conditions.

# Scott and Amundsen

In the race for the Pole, Scott made the fatal mistake of choosing ponies instead of the traditional trained dogs.

The ponies tired fast in the snow and soon had to be put down.

In 1772 Captain James Cook sailed round Antartica, proving that it was unapproachable due to the pack-ice which surrounded it. In 1841 James Clark Ross penetrated the ice barrier with specially designed ships. He discovered a chain of mountains and even an active volcano, Erebus.

In 1909 two expeditions to Antartica got under way. One was led by the Norwegian, Roald Amundsen, who had already found the Northwest passage from the Atlantic to the Pacific. The other was led by the Englishman, Robert Falcon Scott, who had been to Antartica in 1901, discovering dry, ice-free valleys.

Amundsen set up his camp in 1910 and during the winter prepared his men and dogs for the trip. His camp

was already 100 kms nearer the Pole than Scott's.

In spring they both set off, covering an average of 30 to 40 kms a day.

Scott and four of his companions arrived exhausted at the Pole on 16 January, 1912, only to find a small tent flying a Norwegian flag, Amundsen had beaten them by a month.

The return journey, 1,300 kms on foot, was tragic. After four weeks Evans was killed by an avalanche. Soon afterwards Oates, suffering from frostbite, insisted on being left behind.

In March the remaining three men, Scott, Wilson and Bowers were trapped in a blizzard without supplies. Their bodies and their notebooks were found several months later.

Scott and his men arriving at the South Pole discovered the tent left behind by Roald Amundsen.

Another expedition joined the race. Lieutenant Naoshi Shirase of the Japanese Navy had planned to take part in the discovery of the South Pole, but his ships were unable to pass through the pack-ice.

# Our mysterious blue planet

After the discovery of continents new areas of exploration opened up: the depths of the earth and oceans, the summits of mountains, the craters of volcanoes, and the infinite space encircling the globe.

A century ago the importance and complexity of the subterranean world triggered off the new science of pot-holing.

In contrast, scaling the tallest peaks of mountains posed a challenge to climbers. The most famous ascent was recorded in 1953 when Edmond Hillary and the Sherpa Tenzing Norgay reached the summit of Everest.

Closely allied to mountaineering is the science of volcanology. Men dressed in special protective clothing make descents into craters.

Thanks to the amazing progress made in underwater exploration this century tangible evidence has been found to support the theory of continental drift.

Jacques Cousteau, the famous deep-sea diver, pioneered marine archaeology and helped to invent the aqualung in 1943. He has popularised the marvels of the 'silent world' in his many underwater films.

As for the exploration of space it has been a race between the Russians and the Americans. In 1961 the Soviet cosmonaut, Yuri Gagarin, completed an orbital flight around the earth in 108 minutes. He was the first person to see the complete planet and the sun rise twice in one day. The first men on the moon were the three American crew of the US *Apollo* in 1969.

The beauty of the underwater world has been made accessible by television.

*You can see the courses of rivers, and oceans, and details of an astounding precision. The most dominant colour is blue which gets darker and darker around the planet and then comes the white of clouds.*

Yuri Gagarin

# An A to Z of Exploration

**Archaeology**
The study of ancient civilizations.

**Amazons**
A race of women warriors in ancient Greek mythology. It is still not known whether they truly existed, but they appear in the legends of many civilizations.

**Buddha**
The Indian prince Siddharta Gautama gave up his royal destiny to search for Truth. His disciples developed his teachings into a religion which spread throughout Asia: Buddhism.

**Cannibal**
This is a deformation of the Spanish word *caribal*, used for the Indians of the Caribbean islands. They used to eat their enemies in order to acquire their skills and fighting abilities.

**Canoe**
A light boat made of stretched hides sown onto a wooden frame used by Amerindian people.

**Colonization**
This is the exploitation of a land and people by new arrivals. Many voyages of discovery were made for this purpose, armies being sent out to acquire land and wealth for the King. Often the original inhabitants were forced into slavery and made to give up their customs and religion. Many countries which were colonized in the past have only achieved independence this century and are still labouring under the weight of years of exploitative rule.

**Desert**
The word comes from the Latin and means abandoned – a place hostile to all form of life. Deserts have long fascinated explorers, though they can pose grave dangers.

**Despoil**
To plunder. The *conquistadores*, for example, wanted to take the fabulous wealth of the Indians for themselves.

**Ethnography**
The study of a people: their languages, religions, etc.

**Exotic**
Used to describe something unusual and attractive from abroad.

**Fevers**
Many explorers suffered from and even died of fevers caused by tropical diseases such as malaria.

**Gaucho**
An Argentinian cowboy.

**Geology**
The study of the history and structure of the Earth.

**Hydrography**
The study of rivers, lakes and coasts.

**Indigenous**
The original or native inhabitants of a place.

**Jesuits**
Founded in 1540, the religious order of the Jesuits set up missions around the world. Their accounts of their journeys were precious documents for all the scholars interested in the discovery of the world.

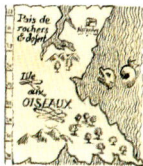

**Khan**
Mongol prince or ruler.

**Lama**
Buddhist priest or monk in Mongolia and Tibet. Their leader is the Dalai Lama.

**Marabout**
In Islamic countries this is the name of a sage of pious man.

**Nile**
The search for the source of the Nile led to many African expeditions (Burton, Speke, Livingstone, Stanley).

**Orient**
The East. The word comes from the Latin meaning 'where the sun rises'.

**Pilgrimage**
A journey to a holy place or shrine, often to ask for guidance.

**Pygmy**
Since ancient times people have spoken of the tiny people who lived by the source of the Nile. In fact, the real pygmies live in the equatorial forest of central Africa.

**Razzia**
An attack on a tribe in order to pillage their livestock and take slaves.

**Religion**
Missionaries often went on expeditions of discovery. They hoped to be able to teach the natives about the Christian god. However, the peoples they met usually had firm beliefs of their own. Force was sometimes used to ensure their conversion.

**Royal Geographical Society**
Founded in 1830 to support and encourage geographical exploration. It gave financial assistance to many explorers of Africa, such as Livingstone.

**Scurvy**
A disease which many sailors suffered from on long journeys. It is due to lack of fresh fruit and vegetables and leads to swollen gums and tiredness.

**Steppes**
Vast grassy plains on which no trees grow. In South America they are called the Pampas; in the United States the Prairies; in Siberia the Taiga.

**Slave Trade**
Whole populations were captured and sold to traders who took them to work on plantations in other countries.

**Trade**
Voyages of discovery were often undertaken in order to open up new trade routes.
    Travellers to the Far East brought spices to Europe and many of the most common vegetables used today, such as tomatoes and potatoes, were brought from South America by the *conquistadores*.

Tibet yaks are used for transport, as opposed to camels, because they can stand the cold conditions better.

**Yak**
A long-haired domesticated bovine from Tibet. At high altitudes in China and

**Yurt**
Mongol tent made of felt stretched over a circular wooden frame.

**Zanzibar**
An island in the Indian Ocean off the coast of Africa, the departure point for many expeditions.

# THE DISCOVERY OF THE WORLD

Collect the other 3 volumes in this series,
each one with beautiful illustrations
by François Place

**Vol. 1: Conquerors and Invaders**
**Vol. 2: Navigators and Explorers**
**Vol. 4: Merchants and Traders**